8-2200

MW00975382

To Our First
    We don't know your
name or if you are a little
boy or a little girl, but we
love you already! And God
loves you.

                Love,
                Nana &
                    Papa
                Grandmama
                    &
                Grandpa

Jesus Teaches Me KINDNESS

The Good Samaritan

The Father Who Forgave

Jon and the Little Lost Lamb

An ARCH BOOKS Gift Collection

*An Inspirational Press Book
for Children*

Previously published as:
THE GOOD SAMARITAN, Copyright © 1964 by Concordia Publishing House
THE FATHER WHO FORGAVE, Copyright © 1983 by Concordia Publishing House
JON AND THE LITTLE LOST LAMB, Copyright © 1965 by Concordia Publishing House

Library of Congress Catalog
Card Number: 97-77416
ISBN: 0-88486-201-1
Printed in Mexico

First Inspirational Press edition published in 1998.

Inspirational Press, A division of BBS Publishing Corporation
386 Park Avenue South, New York, NY 10016
Inspirational Press is a registered trademark of BBS Publishing Corporation.

Published by arrangement with ARCH® Books, a division of Concordia Publishing House,
3558 S. Jefferson Ave., St. Louis, MO 63118-3968.

THE
GOOD
SAMARITAN

Luke 10:25-37 FOR CHILDREN

Written by Janice Kramer
Illustrated by Sally Mathews

Over in the Holy Land,
so many years ago,
a merchant from Jerusalem
went down to Jericho.
He started out one lovely morn
as dawn began to break;
his little donkey carried
all the things he had to take.

The trip was rather pleasant
as they went down their way;
the merchant thought of all the things
that he would do that day.
He had some goods to trade and sell
and many things to buy;
he hoped to get to Jericho
before the night drew nigh.

But little did the merchant know
that farther down the road
a band of robbers eyed with greed
the little donkey's load.
Alert, with evil hearts, they watched
and waited till at last
the unsuspecting merchant and his beast
were walking past.

The leader of the bandits
gave a terrifying shout,
and with this sign the thugs emerged
and suddenly jumped out.

With great big clubs they beat the man;
they beat him till he bled,
then took his donkey, stole his goods,
and left him almost dead.

A silence settled over all,
the merchant was alone;
he lay there suffering by the road,
and no one heard him moan.
Too weak and dazed to help himself,
all he could do was wait;
would no one come along to help
before it was too late?

But down the road there came a man,
and he was drawing near;
at last the bleeding merchant thought
that help was really here!

It was a priest in purple robes,
hands folded as in prayer;
a priest would help the wounded man,
a priest would surely care!

His shuffling footsteps on the road
produced the only sound
while silent was the wounded man
so helpless on the ground.
The priest was busy praying,
his eyes were both shut tight.
But one eye chanced to open
and saw the sorry sight.

"Oh, what a shame!" the priest observed;
"I cannot stop today,
or I'll be late for service.
I must be on my way!
I'm sure that someone will come soon,
so I'll just let him lie."

And carefully
and quietly
he tiptoed right on by.

The merchant was alone again;
was this to be the end?
But then another man came down
the road and round the bend.
He was a Levite,* who helped the priests,
he sure would understand
that here and now he ought to stop
and lend a helping hand.

*A temple assistant

The Levite halted in his tracks,
his eyes grew very wide.
His heart was warm with pity
and felt a pain inside.
He stood there undecided;
he knew he ought to stay,
but what he really wanted was
to turn and run away.

"This truly is a horrid sight,"
the troubled Levite said.
"I really do believe he ought
to be at home in bed.
But I'm no doctor, mercy me,
I might do something wrong!
Besides,

I feel quite sick myself —
I'd better run along."

The day was drawing to an end,
and night was coming on;
the merchant now would surely die,
for every hope was gone.
But as the shadows of the night
displaced the light of day,
another man came down the road
by which the merchant lay.

This man was from Samaria,
his people long had been
despised and hated by the merchant
and all his countrymen.
The chance that this Samaritan
would help was very slim;
he surely wouldn't want to help
a man who hated him!

But as he came around the bend,
he stopped with great surprise;
for when he saw the merchant there,
he hardly could believe his eyes.
"How can it be? This wounded man
is out here all alone;
I would have come here sooner, friend,
if I had only known!"

And then the kind Samaritan
got down upon his knee;
he tried the very best he could
to help his enemy.

He gently bound each bloody wound
and tried to ease the pain;
oh, surely, it would be too bad
if he had helped in vain!

But when he'd given all the help
that he knew how to give,
he saw that now, without a doubt,
the wounded man would live!
He gently placed the merchant on
his donkey's back, and then
the two men and the donkey small
went down the road again.

They had to travel very slow.
It was a lonely night.
At last this kind Samaritan
beheld a welcome sight.

He saw a warm and cozy inn
beside the road ahead;
he took the merchant to the inn
and put him right to bed.

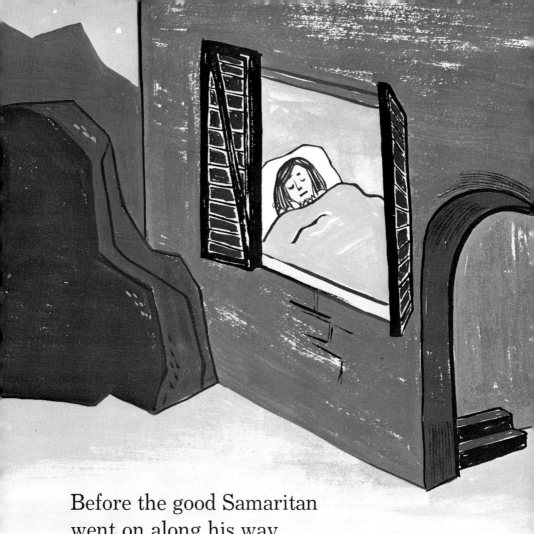

Before the good Samaritan
went on along his way,
he paid the keeper of the inn
to let the merchant stay.
"Be sure to take good care of him," he
    said,
"for I intend
to pay in full, when I return,
for everything you spend."

"Now," asked our Lord,
"*Who* helped his fellowman
in every way he could?
Who was the one who acted here
the way a *neighbor* should?"
The priest, you'll say, was not the one—
he hurried right on by;
nor did the Levite help the man—
he seemed afraid to try.

The good Samaritan—he was
the only one to stay;
and though the merchant hated him,
he helped him anyway.
How wonderful if you and I
and all God's children would
show such a love to all we meet
as Jesus said we should!

Dear Parents:

We are to love our neighbor, the Great Commandment tells us. What does this mean? Does this include people who are not one of us, those of another race and religion, those who look down on us or we on them?

Because people were confused about this, Jesus told our parable. The hero of the story is a member of a people despised and hated by Jesus' nation because the Samaritans' race and religion were not pure.

Can you help your child understand the lesson taught in this parable? Can you help him carry out the sometimes difficult task of being a true neighbor, as the Samaritan was, even to those who may not seem our brothers, our "neighbors"? You may want to read to your child, or help him read it himself, the story of the Good Samaritan in your Bible. (Luke 10:30-37)

THE EDITOR

THE FATHER WHO FORGAVE

Luke 15:11-32 FOR CHILDREN

Written by Robert Baden
Illustrated by Betty Wind

Once long ago and far away
    There lived a wealthy man;
He had two sons; he loved them both
    As much as a father can.

He hoped his boys would both obey
    The laws of God and man;
He prayed that they would live their lives
    According to God's plan.

The older said, "I'll do my best."
    The younger didn't bother;
He said, "I hate to live at home";
    His words upset his father.

This son came where the old man stood
And stared him in the face:
"Please give me half of all you own;
I want to leave this place!"

His father said, "Son, don't forget
   What God and I have told you.
You're old enough to have your way;
   I can no longer hold you."

The older son felt angry when
 His father cried that day:
"I hate the way he's made you sad
 By running off this way!"

His father, though, just sighed and said,
 "Although I'm sad, I love him;
I pray that you'll forgive him too,
 That God will watch above him."

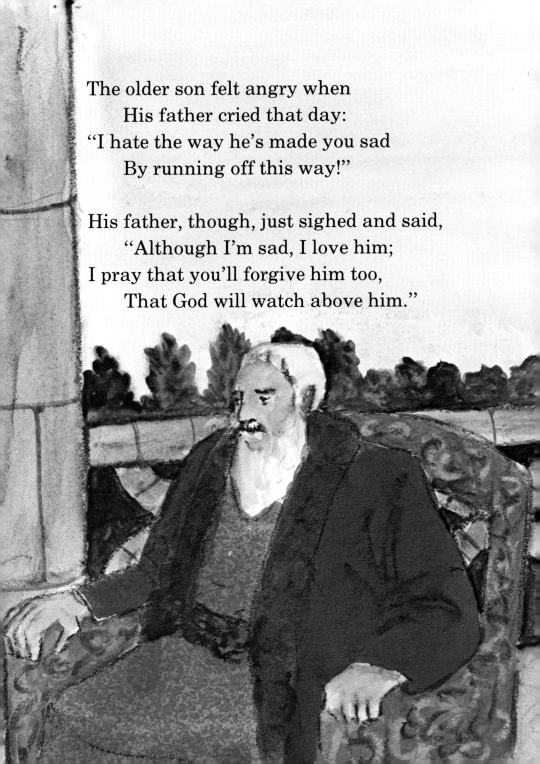

A few weeks later neighbors came
　　With stories of the son:
"He's spending money sinfully;
　　It's shocking what he's done."

This made the father hurt inside;
　　He fell upon his knees;
"Dear God," he prayed, "talk to my son
　　And make him listen. Please!"

Again for weeks he heard no word,
And then he got the news:
"Your son has wasted all he had;
He's even lost his shoes.

"He's feeding pigs to earn enough
    To buy a crust of bread;
It looks to us as if your son
    Might just as well be dead!"

The older brother heard the news
    And said, "I should be sad,
But he is getting what is right
    For wasting what he had."

But once again the father turned
　　To God in prayer then:
"O Lord, please send my boy back home
　　To live with us again.

"I know that what he's done is wrong,
　　But I just can't forget him;
If he would want to come back home,
　　Then surely I would let him."

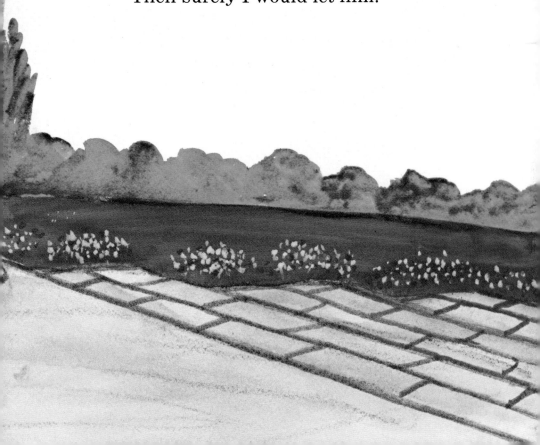

The older brother saw this love
  And heard his father's word;
He shook his head and said, "I can't
  Believe what I've just heard.

"He took your money, ran away,
        And still you think about him;
We've proved that we can run this place
        And get along without him!"

For weeks the father stood upon
    His porch each day and night
To see if he could see his son
    Come walking into sight.

But after watching for an hour,
    He'd come inside once more.
"Perhaps next time," he said, "I'll see
    What I am looking for."

At last far off he saw someone
    And cried, "I see my son!"
He left the porch, went down the steps,
    And broke into a run.

The boy looked tired, dirty, thin;
    His clothes were badly torn;
His shoes were gone, his hair a mess;
    His face looked old and worn.

The boy knelt down and cried, "I've sinned
    And wasted what you gave;
I don't deserve to be your son,
    Please treat me like your slave."

The father didn't scold his son,
    Instead he hugged and kissed him;
He ordered clothes and rings be brought
    And said how much he'd missed him.

He shouted, "Servants, kill a calf,
 The one that looks just right;
Prepare a feast, invite our friends,
 We'll celebrate tonight!"

And soon the banquet was prepared,
    And all sat down to eat;
But where the older brother sat
    There was an empty seat.

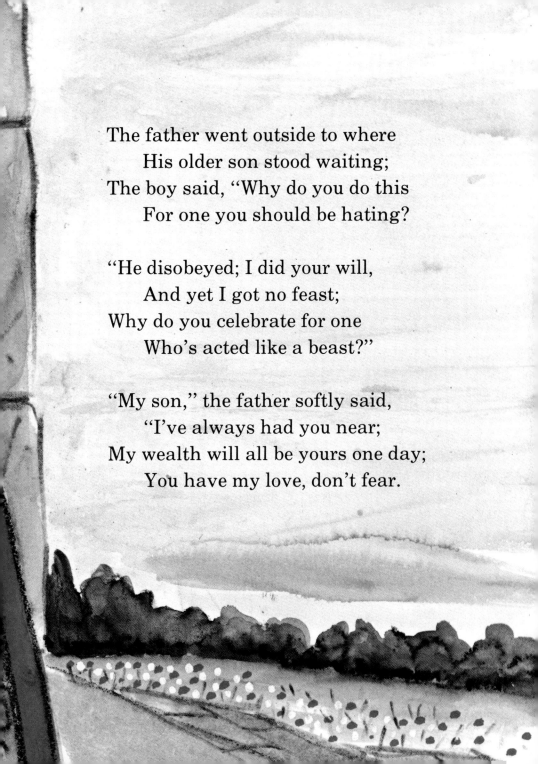

The father went outside to where
    His older son stood waiting;
The boy said, "Why do you do this
    For one you should be hating?

"He disobeyed; I did your will,
    And yet I got no feast;
Why do you celebrate for one
    Who's acted like a beast?"

"My son," the father softly said,
    "I've always had you near;
My wealth will all be yours one day;
    You have my love, don't fear.

"But now your brother has come home;
  It's like he's long been dead;
He lives again, please come inside,
  Don't pout, rejoice instead!"

We don't know what that brother did
  When he heard his father's voice;
He might have gotten mad and left
  Or made some other choice.

But just perhaps he may have learned
  To forgive and love his brother;
If so, they all could celebrate
  In joy with one another.

Dear Parents,

The familiar and beloved story of the Prodigal Son should really be called the parable of the Forgiving Father, for it focuses on the father's forgiving love.

Both sons sinned—the one through gross sins of the flesh, and the other through self-righteousness and love-lessness. The father forgave them both.

The father, of course, represents our gracious God, who forgives sinners of all kinds by virtue of the perfect life and atoning death of His Son Jesus Christ. No one has fallen so low as to be beyond God's reach. Only those who refuse to accept His love make it impossible for Him to save them.

It is essential that your child learn about this great love which the heavenly Father has for him or her. You can help your child to see that through Christ there is forgiveness for those who make "beasts" of themselves as well as for the self-righteous and loveless who are ready to pass harsh judgments on others.

Those who have an understanding of our total dependence on God's gracious love will try to avoid both types of sinning as they trust in His forgiveness through Christ, our Savior.

The Editor

Jon and the Little Lost Lamb

LUKE 15:1-7 FOR CHILDREN

Written by Jane Latourette
Illustrated by Betty Wind

Inside the sheepfold, fast asleep,
What do you see? One hundred sheep!
That little one is "Baby Baa,"
who loves to snuggle in a heap
beside his brothers on the straw.

The morning sun is peeking in
to waken Baby Baa, who's been
a-dreaming of the meadow grass
that grows up where the hills begin,
right near the narrow mountain pass.

Since now another day's begun,
who comes along but Jonathan,
the shepherd, who unlocks the door,
and counts each sheep to see that none
is missing or is sick or sore?

One hundred strong, all safe and sound,
come greet the sun, as out they bound.
And little Baby Baa runs, too,
his tiny hoofs beat on the ground —
until he spies a plant to chew.

The shepherd lets them frisk and play,
before he leads them on their way
to meadows green, quite far from home —
good Jonathan knows every day
just where it's best to graze and roam.

At times it can be dangerous,
as through the narrow mountain
they walk along in single file—

(Now, Baa, don't be so *mischievous!*)
so Jon is watching all the while
to see that wolves aren't waiting there
about to spring down from their lair.

What's that? A lion sees the flock!
The shepherd, with no time to spare,
hurls with his sling a well-aimed rock.

He hits the beast between the eyes.
The lion falls. Stone-still he lies;
he's harmless now. Say, look ahead —
green, juicy grass! Their spirits rise,
and as they eat, Jon has his bread.

His kindly eyes keep in full view
his flock of sheep, who romp and chew,
or rest beneath the big tree's shade.
Let's see what Jon's about to do —
sweet music on the flute he made!

The hours go by, the sun sinks low;
it must be time for them to go
along the path for home again.
The shepherd calls, and in a row
he leads them downhill toward their pen.

They reach the fold, the shepherd counts
the sheep as through the door they bound,
to find a soft spot on the straw.
But wait! Just ninety-nine? He frowns—
oh, *where* is little Baby Baa?

How sad is our good shepherd Jon;
one lamb is lost or strayed. It's gone.
Jon's tired from tending sheep all day —
but he must search up hill and down
and find this lamb who's lost his way.

Jon climbs back to the pasture ground,
keeps calling, looking all around —
until beyond the place they'd stayed
he hears a little bleat that sounds
so low and faint and sore afraid.

You see, this lamb forgot and strayed
from his good shepherd late that day.
He did not hear Jon's call to come
and get in line for walking home,
so Baby Baa just romped and played.

But then he stumbled, tumbled down
into a hole — Would he be found?
The day turned slowly into night;
no shepherd near. What was that sound?
A jackal's howl — Baa froze with fright.

Another sound — his shepherd's voice!
Above the wild beast's night-time noise.
Baa's gently lifted up by Jon;
what happy reason to rejoice!
So safe at last, all fear is gone.

Once back inside the snug sheepfold,
the shepherd does not rant nor scold,
but smooths on olive oil to heal

all Baa's deep scratches, and we're told
it's done so kindly, Baa can feel
How much his shepherd cares for him —
one poor, lost lamb, back home again!

Dear Parents:

Our story is based on Jesus' parable of the Lost Sheep, a companion-story to His parables of the Lost Son and Lost Coin. All of these stories were told by Jesus to explain why He bothered about lost men. (Luke 15:1, 2)

"My attitude is like that of a good shepherd," Jesus says in this parable. God's feelings are just like the shepherd's: he is not satisfied with still having the "ninety-nine." The lostness of the one sheep does not let him rest. His joy over finding a stray sheep is even greater than any satisfaction over his having many sheep who are not lost.

Will you help your child see that Jesus is like the shepherd of our story? That He cares about and loves all God's children, even those who have been bad? That He does not leave them, nor does He want *us* to leave them, to their foolishness but rather brings them back home with joy? He is the "good shepherd Jonathan."

THE EDITOR